D0710296

THE MAJESTIC
Albatross

IMAGES OF KAUA'I'S BELOVED SEABIRDS

Robert Waid

Mutual Publishing

ISBN 1-56647-743-3
Library of Congress Catalog Card Number: 2005928942

First Printing, October 2005
1 2 3 4 5 6 7 8 9

Mutual Publishing, LLC
1215 Center Street, Suite 210
Honolulu, Hawai'i 96816
Ph: 808-732-1709 / Fax: 808-734-4094
Email: mutual@mutualpublishing.com
www.mutualpublishing.com

Printed in Taiwan

Dedication

To the Protectors
Brenda, Cathy, Cindy, Kima, and my beloved Joyce

The author donates all author's royalties to the Kīlauea Point National Wildlife Refuge
to help further the programs to study and protect the albatross.

PREFACE

As you turn the pages of this book and look into the dark brown eyes of this magnificent creature, the Laysan albatross, know that most, if not all, of these birds are, at this moment, hundreds if not thousands, of miles away from us. They are in a world foreign to us humans, a vast seascape in which they masterfully navigate to locate currents, fronts and seamounts that provide squid and fish and other marine creatures on which to feed. Every November some return to land to reacquaint with their lifelong mate and subsequently raise a chick, and others, too young to nest or who have lost a mate, return to socialize and search for a mate. It is during this reproductive period that the human residents of Kaua'i's north shore have the profound privilege of getting a glimpse into the lives of these ocean travelers.

Albatrosses returned to Kaua'i only a few decades ago, and have once again established themselves on lands that their ancestors knew well. They are now a protected species, a mandate much needed for these vulnerable seabirds. The U.S. Fish and Wildlife Service's Kīlauea Point National Wildlife Refuge, located on the north shore of Kaua'i, was established, in part, to conserve and protect albatrosses and other seabirds and their habitat. Unlike their early ancestors (pre-human arrival), today's albatrosses face many dangers while on land, primarily mammalian predators, most often man's best friend. A refuge fence protects nesting seabirds from dogs. Watchful eyes of Bob and his neighbors keep "their" albatrosses safe. Over 500,000 people visit the refuge annually to see these majestic birds, as well as other seabirds, all of which fly over a historic lighthouse that stands on this northernmost point of the inhabited Hawaiian Islands.

Refuge biologists closely monitor the albatross populations on Kaua'i. Several small colonies dot the northern cliffy landscape, but the majority lie within the safety of the refuge. By placing numbered bands on their legs, the history of each bird can be followed year after year. And by placing small tracking instruments on some of the birds, biologists can track where these great wanderers go between island visits.

Bob Waid and his neighbors know each one of the birds that have chosen to nest in their neighborhood. They relish the eight months of the year when they can behold the life cycle that unfolds before them; from the first arriving birds in November that entertain their human observers with their dynamic courtship rituals, egg laying in December, hatching in February, and finally, the fledging of chicks in July. Bob and his neighbors know that these chicks, who must learn to fly and forage on their own, will not return to land for three to four years. During this time, they will learn the art of navigation that their parents know so well. You can bet that Bob and his neighbors will be waiting patiently, albeit anxiously, to see them once again, and watch another generation of Laysan albatrosses soaring the skies of the Garden Isle.

Brenda Zaun, Wildlife Biologist
U.S. Fish and Wildlife Service
Kaua'i National Wildlife Refuge Complex

At length did cross an Albatross,
Through the fog it came;
As if it had been a Christian soul,
We hail'd it in God's name.

It ate the food it ne'er had eat,
And round and round it flew.
The ice did split with a thunder-fit;
The helmsman steer'd us through!

And a good south wind sprung up behind;
The Albatross did follow,
And every day, for food or play,
came to the mariners' hollo!

In mist or cloud, on mast or shroud,
It perch'd for vespers nine;
Whiles all the night, through fog-smoke white,
Glimmer'd the white moonshine.

—*The Rime of the Ancient Mariner*,
by Samuel Taylor Coleridge

INTRODUCTION

Each year in November, the Laysan albatross return to Kaua'i—a lush tropical paradise in the Hawaiian Island chain. After months, sometimes years, at sea, the huge white birds with brown wings touch down on the north shore, an area of steep bluffs overlooking the Pacific Ocean, framed with high waterfalls in the surrounding mountains, accented with Norfolk pines, coconut palms, plumeria trees, African tulip trees, and a wide variety of exotic flowers and shrubs.

The Laysan albatross are among the largest flying seabirds in the world. Weighing an average of twenty-five pounds, they glide on the sea breezes on wings that span six to seven feet. These magnificent birds are so skillful at using the winds and gravity, they can fly thousands of miles in search of food. Their range covers the entire Northern Pacific from the Hawaiian Islands to the subarctic waters near Alaska. By locking their wings into a rigid form, they glide for days at a time, even sleeping while in flight.

Early in the 1900s, man hunted the Laysan albatross for their feathers and gathered their eggs in huge quantities, practices which are now illegal. The population has rebounded to more than one million birds.

Spending 95 percent of their lives on the open ocean, the Albatross visit dry land for one reason—to breed and raise their offspring. The main breeding grounds are the isolated atolls and small islands stringing north of the main uninhabited Islands of Hawai'i—places like Tern Island, Laysan Island, French Frigate Shoals,

Kure Atoll, and Midway. A small percent of Laysan albatross have picked the populated Hawaiian Islands as their nesting grounds. On the north shore of Kaua'i, these beautiful birds breed in the Wildlife Refuge at the Kīlauea Lighthouse, as well as some residential areas. This proximity to public areas allows residents and visitors to view, at a respectful distance, the majestic birds with the fine porcelain-like white feathers on their heads, accented by coal-black eyes. They can enjoy the antics of the adult birds as they strut, dance, clack, waddle, whistle, and moo on the ground, then take to the air to glide effortlessly in figure-eight patterns over the bluffs of the north shore.

Equally as exciting are the baby chicks as they grow from fuzzy balls, just emerged from the egg, into adult-sized chicks, trying out their wings. Many watchers are thrilled by the act of fledging, when the adult-sized chicks are ready to take their first flight out to the open ocean, where they will roam the seas for up to five years before returning to land and starting the mating process.

Most adults, mated for life, will return to the same spot on the Garden Isle in about six months to resume the everlasting cycle. Some adults will take off a year to rebuild their strength for the arduous task of raising a chick.

This collection of photos tells the story of the majestic albatross of Kaua'i through the various stages of their time on land. We are privileged to share the beauty, grace, and joy of the Laysan albatross.

After spending the summer months on the open ocean, the albatross return to Kaua'i in November.

An adult albatross glides effortlessly over the bluffs of the north shore.

These large birds, with wing spans up to seven feet, have a range of
several thousand miles on the open sea.

As well as gliding above the bluffs, they enjoy skimming the waves.

After about five months at sea, the albatross come back to land to mate and raise their young.

On land, the distinctive porcelain-like head feathers and ebony eyes are easily seen.

Forming circles of three to four adults, the albatross often are seen
in a dance of bobbing, clacking, and mooing.

The pairs mate for life, usually returning to the same area each year.

The couples are often seen in seemingly affectionate embraces.

This pair searches for the ideal nesting place. The male and female have the same coloring, the male being slightly larger.

Each pair lays a single egg in a season, generally in early December.

The female in front is sitting on their egg, while the male helps tidy up the nest.

After two months of incubation, the chick emerges by "pipping," or breaking out, the end of the shell.

Only an hour after breaking out of the egg, this chick rests on part of the broken shell.

This one-day-old chick, born in February, is attended by the parent.

During the first several weeks, the parent covers the chick, much like the egg, to keep it dry and warm.

Papa has a good reason to be proud—he shared equally in the egg-sitting duties, often not leaving the nest for weeks.

One parent stays with the chick at all times, while the other is searching for food, then they swap duties.

The chicks begin to check out the neighborhood.

And, they start to grow.

After about two weeks, the adults find they can no longer cover the chick entirely.

This chick doesn't fit any longer.

At the three-week point, the chick is no longer covered, but one parent stays nearby.

This chick, at home under a hibiscus hedge, seems to be listening to words of wisdom.

Then, after about four weeks, the chicks are left alone for the first time, usually for several days at a time.

After long flights to gather fish, squid, and other seafood, the parents rotate the feeding of the chick. The food is predigested for the chick.

After a great meal, mother and chick take a break.

At three months of age, the spikey hairdo gives way to brown fuzz.

Interestingly, each chick stays within fifty yards of where it was hatched, until it is ready to fledge.

This chick, about four months old, has begun to lose the baby fuzz.
Patches of white feathers can now be seen.

And for the first time, the chick starts to exercise its wings.

The chicks are curious about everything—leaves, flowers, and branches.

They appear to enjoy soaking up rays.

Now, more than four months old, the chicks have lost the body fuzz,
showing more of the distinctive adult feathers.

Although almost as big as the adult albatross, the chicks still depend on the parents for food.

They still cannot fly to search for their own food. They are often seen testing out their wings.

Lawn sprinklers seem to be a treat.

By mid-June, at about four-and-a-half months, the head fuzz gives way
to the gleaming white head feathers.

The first powered flight will be on the day the chick fledges, leaving Kaua'i for the open sea.

Getting ready for that day, they occasionally catch a breeze that lifts them off the ground as they test their wings.

At almost five months of age, the chicks experience short test hops.

On the day of fledging, each chick leaves its nest area to walk to the
nearest bluff overlooking the ocean.

This chick has walked to the bluff and is preparing to take its first powered flight from a height of 170 feet above the ocean.

After several hours at the top, the chick takes flight for the first time and heads for the open ocean.

The chicks will remain on the open ocean for several years, before returning to land
when mature enough to start the mating process.

ABOUT THE AUTHOR

Bob Waid has been photographing the Laysan albatross since 1998 when he and his wife, Joyce, moved to the north shore of Kaua'i. They fell in love with these birds when they discovered a baby chick nesting on their property prior to building their new house. During the Hawaiian blessing ceremony at the start of construction, the chick took up a position where the front door would be, a sign of good luck. Construction in that part of the site was delayed until the natural departure of the chick.

Each year, the albatross returned to the same neighborhood to mate and raise their young. Each day throughout the annual process, Waid could see and photograph the activities of the adults and chicks located on their property or nearby residences. Using telephoto lenses from a respectful distance, he collected hundreds of photos. Waid selected the collection of photographs for this book to show the various stages of the albatross' life during their annual return to land.

In addition to photography, Waid does computer-generated 3-D renderings for architectural firms and website design. He also does woodworking, specializing in the use of koa wood, a richly-grained native Hawaiian hardwood.

Born in Kansas City, Waid graduated from the University of Kansas with a BA in psychology. Prior to retirement in 1997, he worked for thirty-five years in the corporate environment, predominantly in the data processing industry. Waid and his wife have a daughter, Natalie, and a son, Michael.